wally jokes for KIDS

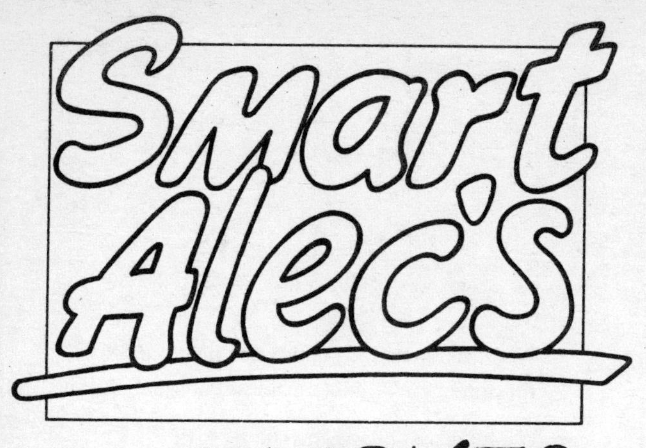

WALLY JOKES FOR KIDS

(OR 101 THINGS TO DO WITH a balloon!)

Illustrated by D. MOSTYN

First published in Great Britain in 1988
by Ward Lock Limited. This edition published
in Great Britain by Beaver Publishing Limited,
Alderley Edge, Cheshire SK9 7DT

Typeset by Columns of Reading
Printed and bound in Finland by UPC Oy

British Library Cataloguing in Publication Data

Smart Alec´s wally jokes for kids.
1. Jokes in English. 1945- – Texts – For children
I. Alec, *Smart*
828´.91402

ISBN 1-85962-008-6

This edition 1997

'My father gave me a musical upbringing — he used to spank me with a violin.'

'How do you catch a squirrel?'
'Climb up a tree and act like a nut!'

Teacher: Why is it that none of you can answer my questions correctly?
Smart Alec: Because, sir, if we could answer them correctly we wouldn't have to be here.

Smart Alec: 'You have a heart of gold.'
Alicia: 'Loving and considerate?'
Smart Alec: 'No, hard and yellow!'

'Did you hear about the dizzy boy scout?'
He spent all day doing good turns.'

'Can you stand on your head?'
'I've tried, but I can't get my feet up high enough.'

'Auntie Maud is rather old. She once went to an antique auction and someone tried to buy her.'

'A man who forgets his wife's birthday is certain to get something to remember her by.'

Post Office Clerk: 'What makes you think you should get a television licence for half price?'
Customer: 'Because I've only got one eye.'

'Dad has a big heart. And he's got a stomach to match.'

'Mum has a soft heart — and a head to match.'

'What's your dad getting for Christmas?'
'Bald and fat!'

HEAD + BOOT = THROB.

'Uncle David's new girlfriend looks like a million — every year of it.'

Vicar: 'What are you going to do when you grow up, young man?'
Smart Alec: 'Grow a beard so I won't have so much face to wash.'

'What were the Chicago gangster's last words?'
'Who put that violin in my violin case?'

'What were Tarzan's last words?'
'Who greased that vine?'

'The more arguments you win the less friends you will have.'

When Aunt Maud came to visit she was very impressed by the attention paid to her by Smart Alec.

'You've been unusually nice to me today, Alec,' she said 'I do believe you don't want me to go.'

'You're right. I don't want you to go auntie,' said Smart Alec, 'Dad says he's going to give me a good hiding when you've gone.'

A newspaper reporter was interviewing a man on his 99th birthday. At the end of the interview the reporter said: 'I hope I can come back to see you next year to help you celebrate your hundredth birthday.'

'I don't see why not,' replied the old man, 'You look healthy enough to me!'

Smart Alec: 'It's a complete waste of time. It's a complete waste of time.'
Dave: 'What is?'
Smart Alec: 'Telling hair-raising stories to my uncle Albert.'
Dave: 'Why's that?'
Smart Alec: 'He's bald.'

Albert: 'Did you enjoy the opera?'
Smart Alec: 'It was all right, apart from the singing.'

Mother: 'Just look at the mess you're in. What on earth have you been doing?'
Smart Alec: 'I fell in a puddle.'
Mother: 'In your new suit?'
Smart Alec: 'I didn't have time to change.'

Judge: 'Order, order, order in the court!'
Prisoner: 'I'll have a ham sandwich and a cup of coffee.'

An idiot spent the evening with some friends but when the time came for him to leave a terrific storm started with thunder, lightning and torrential rain.

'You can't go home in this,' said the host, 'You'd better stay the night.'

'That's very kind of you,' said the idiot, 'I'll just pop home and get my pyjamas.'

'Albert Littleun is so small his chin has a rash from his bootlaces.'

Smart Alec: 'I see your hair is beginning to abdicate.'
Father: 'Abdicate?'
Smart Alec: 'Yes, it's giving up the crown.'

A policeman was amazed to see a hiker walking along the road carrying a signpost which read 'To Brighton'.

'Allo, allo, allo,' said the policeman, 'What are you doing with that?'

'I'm walking to Brighton,' said the hiker, 'And I don't want to lose my way.'

'Henry Uglymug loves nature — in spite of what it did to him.'

Smart Alec: 'Do you believe in free speech?'
Neighbour: 'I certainly do.'
Smart Alec: 'Good, can I use your telephone?'

Useful Advice: 'If your mum's made a cake and you want to lick the beaters on the food mixer, turn off the motor before you do so.'

When Wally Witherspoon proposed to his girlfriend she said: 'I love the simple things in life, Wally, but I don't want one of them for a husband!'

'I beg your pardon,' said the man returning to his seat in the theatre, 'But did I step on your toe as I went out?'

'You certainly did.' the woman replied.

'Oh, good,' said the man, 'That means I'm in the right row.'

Miser: 'How much for a haircut?'
Barber: 'Two pounds.'
Miser: 'How much for a shave?'
Barber: 'One pound.'
Miser: 'Right, shave my head.'

'Have you any blue ties to match my eyes?'
'No, but we've got some soft hats to match your head.'

Old Lady: 'Don't pull faces at that poor bulldog.'
Smart Alec: 'Well, he started it!'

'What's the difference between a sigh, a car and a monkey?'
'A sigh is oh dear.
A car is too dear.
A monkey is you, dear.'

A stupid bank robber rushed into the bank, pointed two fingers at the clerk and said: 'This is a muck-up!'

'Don't you mean a stick-up?' asked the girl.

'No.' said the robber, 'its a muck-up. I've forgotten my gun.'

'Granny is celebrating the 25th anniversary of her 27th birthday.'

Smart Alec: 'I had a funny dream last night, mum.'
Mother: 'Did you?'
Smart Alec: 'Yes, I dreamed I was awake, but when I woke up I found I was asleep.'

'You remind me of the Venus de Milo — beautiful — but not all there.'

'Why don't you go home and brush up on your ignorance?'

Teacher: 'Alec, name the four seasons.'
Smart Alec: 'Salt, pepper, mustard and vinegar.'

'Mum and dad have had a very happy marriage — now and then.'

'Arnold Thislethwaite is so scared of flying he even gets dizzy when he sees an airline ticket.'

'What does your brain want to be when it grows up?'

Teacher: 'Alec, I've taught you everything I know and you're still ignorant.'

Alicia: 'Try some of my sponge cake.'
Smart Alec: 'That's funny. I bought a fresh sponge from the chemist specially.'

Father: 'Hello, Alec. Learn anything new at school today?'
Smart Alec: 'Yes, how to get out of lessons by stuffing red ink up my nose.'

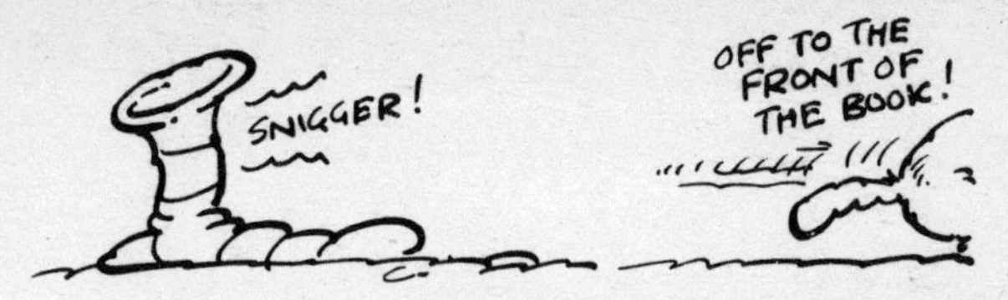

Tramp: 'The lady next door gave me a piece of her homemade cake. Will you give me something?'
Woman: 'How about an indigestion tablet?'

'Have you heard about the latest car? It has a glass floor — so when you run over someone you can see who it was.'

'There's only one thing that prevents dad from being happily married — mum.'

'What did the speak-your-weight machine say when the fat lady stepped on it?'
'One at a time, please!'

Useful Advice: 'To avoid burning your hands in hot water feel the water before putting your hands in.'

'Alec, you mustn't pull the dog's tail.'
'I'm not. I'm only holding it. He's doing the pulling.'

Useful Advice: 'Always borrow money from pessimists. They don't expect to be repaid.'

Mother: 'You always want your own way.
Smart Alec: 'Well, if it's mine, why not give it to me?'

Wife: 'You're always saying you'd die for me, but I notice that you never do.'

'Every morning I shadow box. Today I won.'

Smart Alec: 'Your teeth are like the stars.'
Girlfriend: 'Sparkling and romantic?'
Smart Alec: 'No, they come out at night.'

'The aeroplanes used by Claptout Airways are so old they have outside toilets.'

'The best way to lose a friend is to tell him something for his own good.'

'Buses are so crowded these days the only way to be sure of getting a seat is to become a bus driver.'

'Mum has just got a super fur coat. She bought it for herself for dad's birthday.'

'Sonia Stringbean is so thin if she stands sideways in class the teacher marks her as absent.'

Mother: 'Alec, you are a naughty boy. When Charles threw stones at you why didn't you come and tell me instead of throwing stones back at him?'
Smart Alec: 'What's the point, mum? You know you can't throw for toffee.'

Smart Alec: 'I think grandma needs glasses.'
Mother: 'What makes you say that, Alec?'
Smart Alec: 'Because she's in the kitchen watching the washing machine.'
Mother: 'What's wrong with that?'
Smart Alec: 'She thinks she's watching the wrestling on television.'

Smart Alec (to girlfriend): 'Your cheeks are like peaches — football peetches.'

'I wouldn't say you were thick but if there's an idea in your head it's in solitary confinement.'

'*You ought to be painted in oils.*'
'Why, because I'm so beautiful?'
'*No, because you've got a face like a sardine.*'

'Why don't you go home, your cage should be cleaned out by now.'

Alicia: 'Mum, Alec called me stupid!'
Mother: 'Alec! Tell your sister you're sorry.'
Smart Alec: 'I'm sorry you're stupid.'

'My auntie Maud had so many candles on her last birthday cake all her party guests got sunburnt.'

Smart Alec: 'Your ears are like petals.'
Girlfriend: 'Passion flower petals?'
Smart Alec: No, bicycle petals!

Smart Alec: 'Dad, the vicar says we're all here to help others.'
Father: 'That's right, son.
Smart Alec: 'Then what are the others here for?'

'Look at that bald man over there. It's the first time I've seen a parting with ears.'

'Did you hear about the idiot from Brighton who tried to diddle British Rail?'

'He bought a return ticket to London and didn't go back to Brighton!'

Useful Advice: 'When arguing with a stupid person, be sure that he isn't doing the same.'

Father: 'Who gave you that black eye?'
Smart Alec: 'Nobody gave it to me. I had to fight for it.'

A woodpecker was pecking a hole in a tree. All of a sudden a flash of lightning struck the tree to the ground. The woodpecker looked bemused for a moment and then said: 'Gee, I guess I don't know my own strength!'

Mother: Alec, how did your clothes get all torn?
Smart Alec: 'I tried to stop a boy getting beaten up.'
Mother: 'Oh, who?'
Smart Alec: 'Me.'

Useful Advice: 'If you don't want to be murdered never go into an antique shop and ask "What's new?"'

During the school holidays Smart Alec went to a local farm and said to the farmer: 'Can you use me on the land?'
'No,' said the farmer, 'We have special stuff for that.'

'Did you hear about the stupid motorist who always drove his car in reverse? It was because he knew the Highway Code backwards.'

'What's the most important thing to remember in chemistry?'

'Never lick the spoon.'

Don (on telephone): 'Hello, this is Don. Can you lend me fifty pounds.'
Ray: 'I'm sorry, I can't hear you.'
Don: 'I said can you lend me fifty pounds?'
Ray: 'I can't hear you — there must be a fault on the line.'
Operator (interrupting): 'There's no fault on the line. I can hear him quite clearly.'
Ray: 'Well you lend him the fifty pounds then!'

Smart Alec: 'Mum, can I play the piano?'
Mother: 'Not until you've washed your hands. They're filthy.'
Smart Alec: 'That's all right, mum. I'll just play the black notes.'

'When you leave school you ought to become a bone specialist. You've certainly got the head for it.'

Fred: 'How's your new girlfriend?'
Smart Alec: 'I think we'll be very happy.'
Fred: 'What makes you think that?'
Smart Alec: 'She adores me and so do I.'

An idiotic labourer was told by an equally idiotic foreman to dig a hole in the road.

'And what shall I do with the earth, sir?' asked the labourer.

'Don't be daft, man,' replied the foreman, 'Just dig another hole and bury it.'

Smart Alec: 'May I have a glass of water?'
Mother: 'Thirsty, are you?'
Smart Alec: 'No, I want to see if my neck leaks.'

'Some girls who are the picture of health are just painted that way.'

'What's the difference between a Peeping Tom and someone who's just got out of the bath?'
'One is rude and nosey. The other is nude and rosy.'

'How do you like my new toupee?'
'It looks great. You can't tell it's a wig.'

'Every time I take my girlfriend out for a meal she eats her head off.'
'She looks better that way.'

'We had sponge cake for tea yesterday. Mum sponged the flour from the woman next door . . . the milk from our landlady . . . and ten pence for the gas from the Avon lady.'

'My dad thinks he wears the trousers in our house — but it's always mum who tells him which pair to put on.'

'My little brother is so inquisitive . . . he wanted to take his nose apart to see what makes it run.'

'Waiter, you're not fit to serve a pig!'
'I'm doing my best, sir.'

'How do you recognise a stupid pirate?'
'He's got a patch over each eye.'

'My sister was in last year's pantomime, Aladdin. They used her mouth for the cave.'

First Old Man: 'Almost all our friends are gone, but I miss Frank the most.'
Second Old Man: 'Why Frank?'
First Old Man: 'Because I married his widow.'

'Dolphins are so intelligent that after only a few weeks they can train a man to stand on the edge of the pool each day and throw them fish.'

Tourist (in dockland): Can you direct me to the urinal?
Docker: How many funnels has it got?

Patient: 'Tell me honestly, how am I?'
Dentist: 'Your teeth are fine — but your gums will have to come out.'

An irate woman burst into the baker's shop and said: 'I sent my son in for two pounds of biscuits this morning but when I weighed them there was only one pound. I suggest you check your scales.'

The baker looked at her calmly for a moment or two and then replied: 'Madam, I suggest you weigh your son.'

Smart Alec and his friend went fishing one bright summer's day. They went to their favourite spot on Lord Bumworthy's estate but were soon spotted by the gamekeeper.

'You're not allowed to fish here,' he yelled, 'Didn't you see that notice?'

'Yes.' replied Smart Alec, 'But it said "Private" at the top so I didn't like to read any further.'

'Waiter, how long have you worked here?'

'Six months, sir.'

'Well, it can't have been you who took my order.'

Did you hear about the idiot who was discharged from the submarine service? — He was caught sleeping with the windows open.'

Smart Alec: 'Dad, I think you're wanted on the telephone.'
Father: 'What makes you think that?'
Smart Alec: 'Because the man at the other end said, "Hello, is that you, you old idiot?"'

Mother: 'You were well behaved in church today.'
Smart Alec: 'Yes, when that man offered me a whole plate of money I said, no, thank you.'

My doctor says that I can't play golf.'
'So he's played with you as well has he?'

Crook: 'Stick 'em down!'
Bank Clerk: 'Don't you mean "Stick 'em up"?'
Crook: 'No wonder I don't make any money.'

'You should get a job in the meteorology office.'
'Why?'
'Because you're an expert on wind.'

She's so fat it's embarrassing to go shopping with her. She's always being searched by store detectives. They can't believe all those lumps and bumps are hers.

'We've got a welcome mat at home. On the underside is "Clear Off" for unwelcome visitors.'

'She's the kind of girl that boys look at twice — they can't believe it the first time.'

'I can't understand why people say my girlfriend's legs look like matchsticks. They do look like sticks — but they certainly don't match.'

'An adult is a person who has stopped growing at both ends and started growing in the middle.'

'My new girlfriend has got a face like a seaside hotel in November . . . a vacant look.'

When the vicar called at the house Smart Alec was asked to take him a glass of sherry. He handed it to the vicar and then stood watching. 'What is it, my son?' asked the vicar.

'I'm waiting to see you do your trick.' said Smart Alec.

'What trick is that?' asked the reverend gentleman.

'Well, dad says you drink like a fish.'

Smart Alec: 'I didn't like that pie.'
Cook: 'What! I'll have you know that I was making pies before you were born.
Smart Alec: 'I think that was one of them.'

'You could describe my dad as a Conservative-Liberal. He's conservative with his money but liberal with anyone else's.'

Reporter: To what do you attribute your old age?
Grandad: To the fact that I was born a long time ago.

Diner: This food is terrible. I want to see the manager.
Waiter: I'm sorry but you can't see him at the moment. He's out to lunch!

A bore is someone who wants to tell you about himself when you want to tell him about yourself.

Smart Alec: 'Can I have a pie, please?'
Cook: 'Do you want anything with it?'
Smart Alec: 'Yes, if it's anything like the one I had yesterday I'd better have a hammer and chisel as well.'

Teacher: 'I don't look thirty-five do I?'
Smart Alec: 'No, but I bet you did when you were.'

'Did you hear about the businessman who is so rich he has two swimming pools, one of which is always empty? It's for people who can't swim.'

'That boy is so dirty the only time he washes his ears is when he eats water melon.'

'My grandad has so many wrinkles on his forehead he has to screw his hat on.'

Fred: 'I was sorry to hear that your mother-in-law had died. What was the complaint?'
Ted: 'We haven't had any yet.'

'My friend is so stupid he thinks twice before saying nothing.'

The bride was so ugly the groom kissed the bridesmaid.

Waiter: 'We've got just the meal for idiots like you.'
Diner: 'What's that?'
Waiter: 'Chump chops.'

Teacher: 'How old do you think I am?'
Smart Alec: 'I don't know, but you don't look it.'

'They've dug up our street so often it would be cheaper to equip the road with a zip.'

'My sister is so dim she thinks that a cartoon is a song you sing in a car.'

Fred: 'Are you trying to make a fool of me?'
Smart Alec: 'Oh no, I never interfere with nature.'

Baby Bear: 'Who's been eating my porridge and eaten it all up?'
Father Bear: 'And who's eaten my porridge?'
Mother Bear: 'Don't be so stupid, I haven't made it yet!'

'He could be an even bigger idiot but he lacks ambition.'

'My wife has a slight impediment in her speech. Every so often she has to stop to breathe.'

A woman woke her husband in the middle of the night. 'There's a burglar downstairs eating that cake I made this morning.'
'Who shall I call?' said the husband, 'Police or ambulance?'

'Dad is ashamed to be wearing last year's suit. He was ashamed to wear it last year, too.'

'You're so fastidious.'
'You mean I'm discriminating?'
'No, you're fast and hideous.'

A question for husbands: 'Did you wake up with a grouch this morning? Or did she wake up before you?'

'You are such a mess, you look like an accident waiting to happen.'

Mother: 'Eat up your spinach, it'll put colour in your cheeks.'
Smart Alec: 'Who wants green cheeks?'

Doctor: 'There's nothing wrong with you, madam. You just need a rest.'
Woman: 'But look at my tongue!'
Doctor: 'Yes, that needs a rest as well.'

'My mother is so stupid she thinks a string quartet is four people playing tennis.'

'What's the cure for water on the brain?'
'A tap on the head.'

'Being overweight is like putting sugar in coffee . . . after a while it all settles on the bottom.'

Wife: 'I'm going back to mother.'
Husband: 'Well, that's better than her coming back here.'

'Sometimes we moan about mum's cooking but dad is such a bad cook he even burns corn flakes.'

Fred: 'Why do you want to be buried at sea?'
Ted: 'Because my wife has promised to walk on my grave.'

Smart Alec: 'Do babies come from Heaven?'
Father: 'Of course they do.'
Smart Alec: 'Fancy leaving Heaven for a place like this.'

'They've put sand on our local football pitch. It's to stop the team slipping out of the league.'

Teacher: 'What is snow?'
Smart Alec: 'Well-dressed rain.'

'Did you hear about the wally who tried to iron his curtains? He fell out of the window.'

Thin Girl: 'How are your violin lessons going?'
Fat Girl: 'Oh, I've given them up.'
Thin Girl: 'Why is that?'
Fat Girl: 'Well, my music teacher said I should rest the violin against my chin — and I couldn't decide which one.'

'Dad is so keen on cricket he even married an old bat.'

Granny: 'If you don't eat your cabbage you won't grow up to be a beautiful lady.'
Alicia: 'Didn't you eat your cabbage, Granny?'

Teacher: 'What is pop art?'
Smart Alec: 'That's what my dad says when he's going to pop-art for a quick one down the pub.'

Smart Alec: 'Did you know that my sister likes fishing?'
Fred: 'No, is she a keen angler?'
Smart Alec: 'Oh, she doesn't fish for fish, she fishes for compliments.'

Smart Alec: 'I can sell you something for 10p that cost me 20p and I'll still make a profit.'
Mike: 'All right here's my 10p. What is it?'
Smart Alec: 'A used bus ticket.'

Smart Alec: 'Dad, why do you like watching the silent films on television?'
Father: 'Because there's something wonderful about seeing a woman open her mouth and not having a word reach my ears.'

'My wife and I were happy for fifteen years — and then we met.'

'My dad is so bald he combs his hair with a sponge.'

Willy: 'What time is it?'
Wally: 'I've no idea.'
Willy: 'I know that but what's the time?'

Barney Beanpole is so tall he has to stand on a chair to comb his hair.

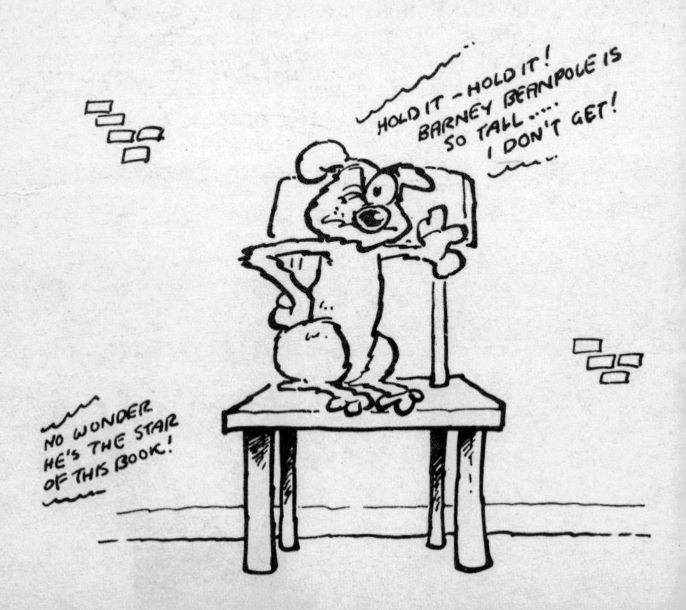

'A firm of furniture dealers claim they can take a modern suite and in a week treat it so it appears to be genuine antique. That's nothing. Smart Alec can do it in ten minutes.'

Never envy a rich man. A rich man is nothing but a poor man with money.

Teacher: 'Why did you go for a haircut in school time?'
Smart Alec: 'It grew in school time.'
Teacher: 'Not all of it.'
Smart Alec: 'I didn't have it all cut off.'

Fiona: 'What's your new boyfriend like?'
Shona: 'He's ugly, he's mean, he's dirty . . . and those are just his good points.'

'At school Joey is teacher's pet. She puts him in a cage at the back of the class.'

Smart Alec: 'Mum made a silly mistake this morning. She gave dad soap flakes instead of corn flakes for breakfast.'
Fred: 'Was he mad?'
Smart Alec: 'He foamed at the mouth.'

'Why do idiots eat biscuits?'
'Because they're crackers.'

'Why did the robot act stupid?'
'Because he had a screw loose.'

Useful Advice: 'Never borrow money from an optimist. He'll expect to get it back.'

One day Smart Alec heard his parents talking. They were discussing what they wanted to do with him. Fortunately for him there's a law against it.

Smart Alec: 'I think you should join the FBI.'
Charlie: 'Federal Bureau of Investigation?'
Smart Alec: 'No, Feather Brained Idiots.'

Smart Alec: 'I had an argument with my girlfriend yesterday. I wanted to go to the zoo and she wanted to go to the ballet.'
Bert: 'Oh, and so what was the ballet like, then?'

A rather stout lady asked Smart Alec if he could see her across the road.

'I could see you a mile away.' said Alec.

An idiot was examining a broken window. He looked at it for a while and then said: 'It's worse than I thought. It's broken on both sides.'

Smart Alec: 'Dad, if I plant this pip in the garden will it grow into an orange tree?'
Father: 'It might do, Alec.'
Smart Alec: 'That's funny — it's a lemon pip.'

'Yes, I do like your dress — but isn't it a little early for Hallowe'en?'

'Mum's cooking is improving. The smoke is not as black as it used to be.'

Joan's teacher got so fed up of her fooling around in class that he wrote a letter of complaint to her father.

'What's all this about?' roared dad, 'Your teacher says he finds it impossible to teach you anything.'

'I told you he was no good.' said Joan.

'When my girlfriend goes out riding she looks like part of the horse. When she dismounts she still looks like part of the horse.'

Actor: 'In that death scene of mine, I moved the audience to tears.'
Critic: 'That's because they knew you were only pretending.'

Visitor: 'Your dog's not very friendly. Every time I eat some of my dinner he growls at me.'
Smart Alec: 'That's probably because you're eating out of his bowl.'

'My mother is such a bad driver that the traffic lights turn white when they see her coming.'

Mother: 'Why are you spanking Jimmy?'
Father: 'Because he's getting his school report tomorrow and I won't be here.'

Diner: 'Have you got asparagus?'
Waiter: 'No, we don't serve sparrows and my name's not Gus.'

Boy: 'Are you a good sculptor?'
Visitor: 'What makes you think I'm a sculptor.'
Boy: 'Well, dad said you were a dirty chiseler.'

First Wally: 'I'll meet you in the town square.'
Second Wally: 'OK. But how will I know you're there?'
First Wally: 'I'll put a chalk mark on the pavement.'
Second Wally: 'That's a good idea. And if I get there first I'll rub it out.'

He is such a bore. The only thing his conversation needs is a little lockjaw.

'Answer the 'phone.'
'It's not ringing.'
'Why leave everything to the last minute?'

'My dad says he never knew happiness until he got married — then it was too late.'

'I can't get over that new beard of yours. It makes your face look like a busted sofa.'

Magician: 'Will someone please call out any number between ten and twenty?'
Spectator: 'Seventeen.'
Magician: 'Thank you. I just wanted to see if anyone was still awake.'

Twit: 'When you were in Paris did you see the Venus de Milo?'
Twit 2: 'See her? I shook hands with her.'

Knock! Knock!
Who's there?
'Sonia.'
'Sonia who?'
'Sonia foot, I can smell it from here.'

'My dad deserves a great deal of credit for his position in life today. He's a self-made nobody.'

'What's the difference between a crossword expert, a greedy boy, and a pot of glue?'
'A crossword expert is a good puzzler and the greedy boy's a pud guzzler. The pot of glue? Ah, that's where you get stuck!'

Mother: 'No, you can't have any more cakes. It's bad for you to go to bed on a full stomach.'
Smart Alec: 'That's all right, mum. I'll lie on my side.'

'Did you hear about the stupid photographer? He saved burned-out lightbulbs for use in his darkroom.'

Smart Alec: 'Dad, the boy next door says I look just like you.'
Father: 'And what did you say?'
Smart Alec: 'Nothing, he's bigger than me.'

'My father suffers from stomach trouble. He can't get his trousers over it.'

Wilberforce Witherspoon saw a notice outside a police station which read: MAN WANTED FOR ROBBERY. So he went in and applied for the job!

'Why is a red-headed idiot like a biscuit?'
'Because he's a ginger nut.'

When he received the end of term report Brenda's father went up in the air. 'This report is terrible,' he said, 'I'm not at all pleased with it.'

'I told the teacher you wouldn't like it,' said Brenda, 'But he insisted on sending it just the same.'

'I can't understand the critics saying that only an idiot would like that television programme . . . I enjoyed it.'

'Bacon discovered the magnifying glass. At our local cafe you need a magnifying glass to discover the bacon.'

'Did you hear about the idiot who invented the one piece jigsaw puzzle?'

Smart Alec: 'Mum, can you wash my face?'
Mother: 'Why can't you wash it yourself?'
Smart Alec: 'Because that'll mean getting my hands wet, and they don't need washing.'

Mother: 'I told you not to have one of those cakes and now there's only one left!'
Smart Alec: 'That's the one I haven't had.'

Ben's new girlfriend uses such greasy lipstick that he has to sprinkle his face with sand to get a better grip.

Fred: 'Why does your wife wear make up but no lipstick?'
Ted: 'She can't keep her mouth still long enough to put it on.'

Two men were discussing their weddings. 'I'll never forget mine, I got a terrible fright,' said the first.

'What happened?' enquired the second.

'I married her,' replied the first.

In the good old days husbands used to come home from work and say: 'What's cooking?' Now they say: 'What's thawing?'

There were two butcher's shops alongside each other in the shopping centre. Outside one was the sign: WE MAKE SAUSAGES FOR THE QUEEN. Outside the other was a sign: GOD SAVE THE QUEEN.

Teacher: 'Where are you from?'
Pupil: 'Wales, miss.'
Teacher: 'Which part?'
Pupil: 'All of me.'

'Did you hear about the wally leaning over the freezer in the supermarket? Five fish fingers reached up and grabbed him by the throat.'

Father: 'What is this?'
Mother: 'It's cottage pie.'
Father: 'I thought so, I've just eaten the door.'

Coach: 'You played a great game, Alec.'
Smart Alec: 'I thought I played rather badly.'
Coach: 'You played a great game for the other side.'

'I reckon mum must be at least thirty years old — I counted the rings under her eyes.'

Teacher: Are you really going to leave school, Ben, or are you just saying that to brighten my day?

'Did you hear about the stupid angler who poured whisky into the river? He thought the fish would come up ready canned.'

Mike: 'My grandad is still alive at the ripe old age of 98.'
Smart Alec: 'That's nothing. My grandpa is still alive at 139.'
Mike: '139?'
Smart Alec: 'Yep, 139 Lettsby Avenue.'

'That girl is so ugly she goes to the beauty parlour on Monday and doesn't come out till Wednesday.'

The dustmen were just about to leave the street when a woman came running out of the house carrying some cardboard boxes. 'Am I too late for the rubbish?' she called.

'No, lady,' replied one of the dustmen, 'Jump right in!'

Roger is so lazy that when he drops something he waits till he has to tie his shoelaces before he'll pick it up.

Mother: 'Alec, eat your dinner.'
Smart Alec: 'I'm waiting for the mustard to cool.'

Two men walked into a pub. The first one went to the bar and said, 'Two pints of beer, please. One for me and one for Donkey.'

The barman turned to the second man and asked: 'Why did he call you Donkey?'

The man replied:'Eeyore, eeyore, eeyore e'always calls me that.'

If beauty is skin deep you must be inside out.

My girlfriend is so ugly she spends three hours a week at the beauty parlour — just to get an estimate!

Girl: 'Did you know that girls are smarter than boys?'
Boy: 'Really? I never knew that.'
Girl: 'See what I mean?'

Wife: 'I'm sorry, dear, but the dog has eaten your dinner.'
Husband: 'Don't worry, we'll go to the pet shop tomorrow and buy a new dog.'

'Why did the lazy idiot apply for a job in the bakery? He fancied a long loaf.'

'My room in our holiday hotel was so small that to walk in my sleep, I had to stand on the bed and mark time.'

Trevor's mother is mad about children . . . she'd have given anything for Trevor to have been one.

Wife: 'Shall I give that tramp one of my cakes?'
Husband: 'Why, what harm has he ever done us?'

Mother: 'There were two cakes in the pantry yesterday and now there's only one. What do you have to say to that?'
Smart Alec: 'It was so dark I didn't see the other one.'

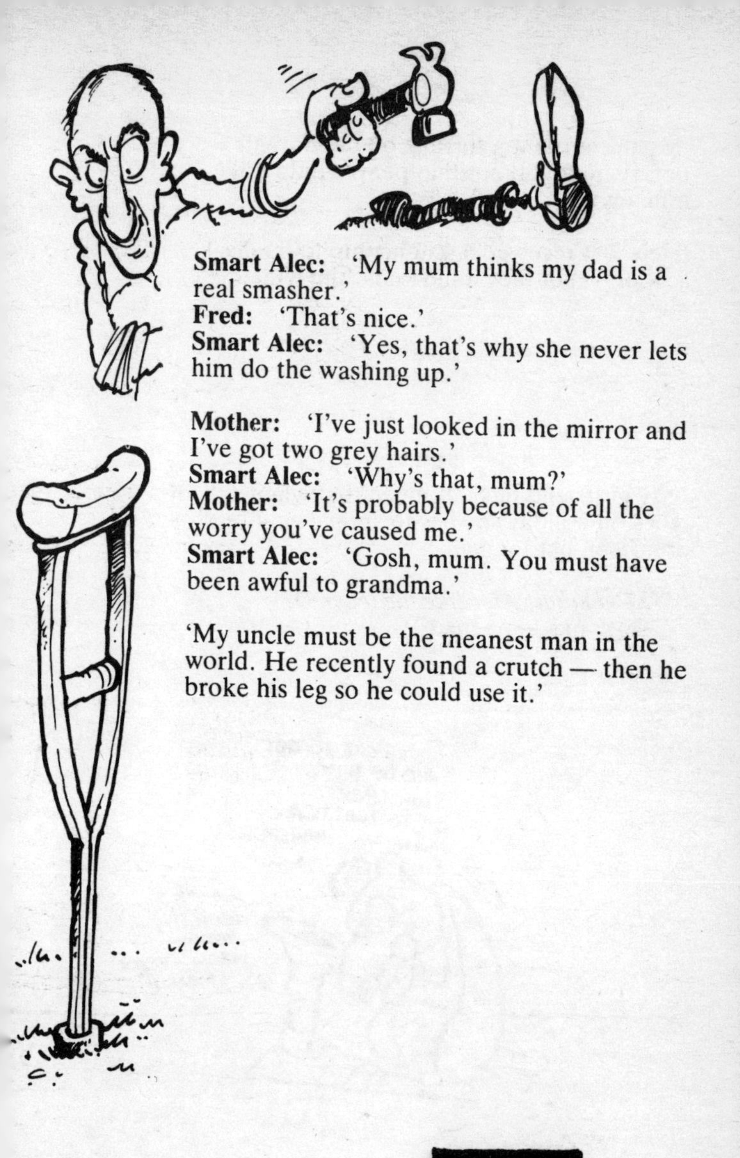

Smart Alec: 'My mum thinks my dad is a real smasher.'
Fred: 'That's nice.'
Smart Alec: 'Yes, that's why she never lets him do the washing up.'

Mother: 'I've just looked in the mirror and I've got two grey hairs.'
Smart Alec: 'Why's that, mum?'
Mother: 'It's probably because of all the worry you've caused me.'
Smart Alec: 'Gosh, mum. You must have been awful to grandma.'

'My uncle must be the meanest man in the world. He recently found a crutch — then he broke his leg so he could use it.'

'My uncle spent a fortune on deodorants before he found out that people didn't like him anyway.'

'He's just received a scholarship to medical school — but they don't want him while he's alive.'

'My girlfriend talks so much that when she goes on holiday she has to spread sunburn lotion on her tongue.'

'Why is Smart Alec like the letter D?'
'Both make ma mad.'

'His name, Wilf, was suggested by his mother. They weren't able to use the name suggested by his father.'

'Did you hear about the millionnaire who had a bad accident? He fell off his wallet.'

'What do you call a stupid spaceman?'
'An astronut.'

Bert: 'I wonder what happened to that stupid blonde woman Fred used to go out with.'
Alice: 'I dyed my hair.'

Smart Alec: 'I'd like a lock of your hair.'
Girl: 'Oh, how romantic. Is that so you'll never forget me?'
Smart Alec: 'No, I'm stuffing a mattress.'

Mother: 'We're having Auntie Mabel for Christmas dinner this year.'
Smart Alec: 'Well, she can't possibly be any tougher than the turkey we had last year!'

George is the type of boy that his mother doesn't want him to associate with.

'Our school cook is so stupid she thinks coq au vin is chicken on a lorry.'

Mike: 'My sister went to a beauty parlour and had her face lifted yesterday.'
Alec: 'Goodness! Who'd want to steal a face like that?'

'When doing exams Dick knows all the answers. It's the questions that get him confused.'

'When I was at school I was as smart as the next fellow. What a pity the next fellow was always an idiot.'

Captain: 'Why didn't you stop the ball?'
Goalie: 'I thought that's what the net's for.'

'They asked my dad to be a blood donor — he's not even a blood owner!'

Smart Alec: 'You're from Scotland, aren't you?'
Iain: 'Aye.'
Smart Alec: 'What does "I dinna ken" mean?'
Iain: 'I don't know.'
Smart Alec: 'Well, if you're Scottish, you ought to!'

Mother: 'Do you always bath in muddy water?'
Smart Alec: 'It wasn't muddy when I got in.'

'Did you hear the story about the dust-cart? It's a load of rubbish.'

'Did you hear about the stupid Australian who received a new boomerang for his birthday? He spent two days trying to throw the old one away.'

Granny: 'You've left all your crusts, Alec. When I was your age I loved the crusts.'
Smart Alec: 'Do you still like crusts, grandma?'
Granny: 'Yes, of course I do.'
Smart Alec: 'Well, you can have mine.'

Father: 'I can't find my computer magazines anywhere. Baby must have thrown them in the fire.'
Mother: 'Don't be silly . . . baby can't read.'

The headmaster looked up at the teacher with a frown on his face. 'Your handwriting is so bad I can't read these examination notes of yours. Why didn't you type them before you gave them to me?'

The teacher became furious, 'Type them?' he yelled, 'If I could type do you think I'd be wasting my time as a teacher?'

Mrs Shufflem: 'My husband is so polite. He always takes his shoes off before he puts his feet on the table.'

Cook: 'Any complaints?'
Smart Alec: 'Yes, these peas are too hard.'
Cook (trying a fork full of peas from Alec's plate?: 'They seem quite soft to me.'
Smart Alec: 'So they should, I've been chewing them for ten minutes.'

'It was so hot when we went on holiday last year that we had to take turns sitting in each other's shadow.'

Bobby was so surprised when he was born he was speechless for eighteen months.

'Why do you always have flat tyres on your bicycle?'

'So I can reach the pedals.'

'The seaside resort we went to last year was so boring that one day the tide went out and never came back.'

'What do you call crazy fleas?'

'Loony ticks.'

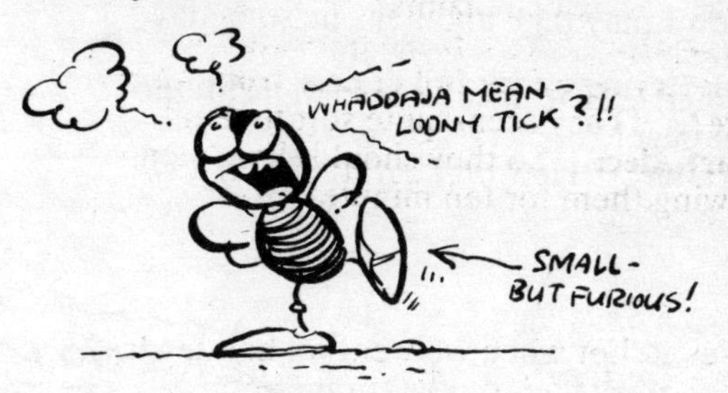

Teacher: 'What do you know about the speed of light?'
Smart Alec: 'It gets here too early in the morning.'

Jane often gets good marks at school. Her and the boy in front never get less than 98%. The boy gets 90 and Jane gets 8.

Jeff had a bath yesterday. As he got in he said to himself: 'Who knows, I might like it, and if I do I may take another one someday.'

Diner: 'This meal is terrible. Call the manager.'
Waiter: 'He won't eat it, either, sir.'

Rosie came into the kitchen holding her stomach and moaning.
'Are you in pain?' asked her mother.
'No, the pain's in me,' Rosie replied.

'My parents were married on Guy Fawkes' Day and it's been fireworks for dad ever since.'

'My dad has trouble with corns. He's bathed his feet in a bowl of corn flakes but they're no better.'

'In our holiday hotel my bedroom was so damp. There was a mousetrap in the corner — with a kipper in it.'

'*Waiter, you've brought me the wrong order.*'
'Well, you said you wanted something different.'

'My teacher is so old even his toupee has turned grey.'

Alec was sitting by the river bank when the gamekeeper came along. 'Can't you see that sign?' he bellowed. 'It says "No Fishing".'
'And it's absolutely right,' said Alec, 'I haven't had a bite all day.'

Smart Alec: 'I'm having a birthday party next week. Would you like to come?'
Mary: 'Yes, please. Where do you live?'
Smart Alec: 'Ten Thatwas Close. Just press the doorbell with your elbow.'
Mary: 'With my elbow? Why can't I press the bell with my finger?'
Smart Alec: 'You're not coming without a present, are you?'

Teacher: 'Why are you late?'
Smart Alec: 'I squeezed my toothpaste too hard this morning and it took me two hours to get it all back into the tube.'

'Waiter, do I have to wait here until I die of starvation?'
'No sir, we close at six o'clock.'

Mother: 'If you've finished your meal say Grace.'
Smart Alec: 'Thanks for the meal, Lord.'
Mother: 'That wasn't much of a Grace.'
Smart Alec: 'It wasn't much of a meal.'

It was decided that there should be a school boxing team and Alec volunteered to join. He got into the ring and spent some time swinging punches but not one hit the other boxer.

At the end of the first round Alec went to the coach and said, 'Do you think I'm going to win?'

'Keep swinging like that,' replied the coach, 'You may win by giving him a cold.'

Father: 'This suit fits me like a glove.'
Smart Alec: 'Pity it doesn't fit you like a suit.'

'What feature runs in your family?'

'Noses.'

'I've got a couple of minutes to kill. Why not tell me everything you know?'

Teacher: 'What are you going to do when you leave school?'
Smart Alec: 'I'm going to join a circus.'
Teacher: 'What are you going to do in the circus?'
Smart Alec: 'I'm going to be a midget.'
Teacher: 'But you're too tall to be a midget.'
Smart Alec: 'That's the idea. I'll be the biggest midget in the world.'

Headmistress: 'What tense is "I am beautiful"?'
Smart Alec: 'Past.'

'Let me look at you for a second. I want to forget you exactly as you are.'

'Did you hear about the two idiots who drowned digging a grave for their friend who wanted to be buried at sea?'

'One of my ancestors died at Waterloo.'
'Really? Which platform?'

'Knock! Knock!'
'Who's there?'
'Major.'
'Major who?'
'Major answer the door.'

Golfer: 'Reverend, do you think it's a sin for me to play golf on a Sunday?'
Vicar: 'The way you play golf it's a sin any day.'

Smart Alec: 'Dad, are slugs nice to eat?'
Father: 'Alec! People do not talk about such revolting things at the dinner table. Ask me later.'
(Later)
Father: 'Now then, Alec. What did you want to know about slugs?'
Smart Alec: 'It doesn't matter any more. There was one on your dinner plate, but it's gone now!'

'At the school speech day the band played Mozart. Mozart lost.'

‘She’s the sort of person who not only makes her guests feel at home but makes them wish they were there too.’

‘It’s pretty tough having to pay £7 for a steak but it’s usually a lot tougher if you pay only £3.’

‘A lady talking about her husband said, “Before we were married he was my ideal, now he’s my ordeal.”’

‘What’s your name?’
‘Milk Bottle.’
‘Why are you called Milk Bottle?’
‘I was found on a doorstep.’

'What do you call a stupid pig thief?'
'A hamburglar.'

A car stopped alongside Bob and the driver said: 'Excuse me, can you tell me where this road goes to?'
'It don't go nowhere,' grinned Alec, 'It stays just where it is.'

Smart Alec: 'Are you superstitious?'
Carl: 'No.'
Smart Alec: 'Then lend me £13.'

'Did you hear about the small man who wanted to work in a bank? Because he was so small they offered him a job in a piggy bank.'

Teacher: 'Take twelve from thirty. What's the difference?'
Smart Alec: 'That's what I say — what's the difference?'

'My dad is so fat he can't play golf because if he puts the ball where he can hit it, he can't see it and if he puts the ball where he can see it he can't hit it.'

Girl: 'Do you say I'm like a dove because I'm soft and cooing?'
Boy: 'No, because you've got pigeon toes.'

Vicar: 'I saw you pick up an apple in the greengrocer's. But I was very pleased to see you put it back. Was that because your conscience told you it was wrong?'
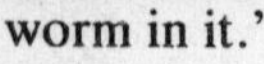
Smart Alec: 'No, it was because it had a worm in it.'

THEY EVEN INSULT WORMS.... SOB!!

'What is worse than finding a worm in an apple?'
'Finding half a worm.'

'My friend is such a wally. He once drove his car into the sea because he wanted to dip his headlights.'

'Why are you so angry?'
'It's all the rage.'

Teacher: 'You can't sleep in class.'
Smart Alec: 'I could if you didn't talk so loud.'

Diner: 'If this is venison, I'm an idiot.'
Waiter: 'Yes, sir it is venison.'

'He's the only person I know who brightens a room when he goes out.'

Bus Passenger: 'Am I all right for the zoo?'
Bus Conductor: 'By the look of you I'd say yes — but I'm a conductor not a zoologist.'

Smart Alec: 'Dad, are you growing taller all the time?'
Father: 'No, why do you ask?'
Smart Alec: 'Because the top of your head is poking up through your hair.'

The inspector boarded the bus and went upstairs to the top deck. 'Tickets, please!' he called.

Alec held out his ticket and the inspector looked at it rather suspiciously. 'And where did you get on?' he asked.

'Downstairs,' said Alec.

'What is a stupid ant?'

'An ignorant.'

Vera: 'I'm sorry I can't come to your party tomorrow. I'm going to see Romeo and Juliet.'

Nora: 'That's all right. Bring them along, too.'

First Schoolboy: 'Will you donate 10p to bury a teacher?'
Second Schoolboy: 'Here's 50p — bury five of 'em.'

Harold Wishbone is the sort of person that you don't like when you first meet him. But once you get to know him you grow to hate his guts.

Mrs Jones: 'I've just come from the beauty parlour.'
Mrs Smith: 'Too bad they were closed.'

'My sister is so dim she thinks an operetta is a girl that works on a telephone switchboard.'

'People don't like me at first but then I get to grow on them.'

'So that's why they call you a little wart!'

Mrs Smith: 'I felt kind-hearted this morning so I gave a tramp a pound.'
Mrs Jones: 'That was good of you but what did your husband say about it?'
Mrs Smith: 'Thanks very much!'

Mother: 'You were a long time coming. Didn't you hear me calling you?'
Smart Alec: 'No, mum — not until you called for the fourth time.'

Smart Alec: 'Mum, where's my oesophagus?'
Mother: 'I don't know. If you kept your room tidy you'd be able to find things when you want them.'

Girl: 'Where are we going to eat?'
Boy: 'Let's eat up the road.'
Girl: 'Oh, no. I don't like asphalt.'

Mrs Smith: 'What's your son going to be when he finishes his education?'
Mrs Jones: 'Old.'

Barber: 'Your hair needs cutting badly.'
Smart Alec: 'Well go ahead. You cut it badly last time.'

'Your little mind must feel very lonely in such a big head.'

Mother: 'How did you like that cake I baked?'
Father: 'It was terrible.'
Mother: 'Don't be silly. The cook book says it's delicious.'

Mrs Smith: 'I'm told you have a model husband.'
Mrs Jones: 'That's true — but unfortunately he's not a working model.'

'My father trains monkeys.'
'Can you do any tricks?'

Golfer: 'Caddy, why do you keep looking at your watch.'
Caddy: 'It's not a watch, it's a compass.'

Father: 'I never told lies when I was a boy.'
Smart Alec: 'When did you start?'

'My big brother is such an idiot. The other day I saw him hitting himself on the head with a hammer. He was trying to make his head swell so his hat wouldn't fall over his eyes.'

KOMPETISHUN KORNER

'I'm as fit as a fiddle.'
'You look more like a cello.'

First Man: 'And this is your most charming wife?'
Second Man: 'No, she's the only one I've got.'

Mother: 'I've made the chicken soup.'
Smart Alec: 'Thank goodness for that. I thought it was for us.'

Girl: 'The man I marry must be a hero.'
Boy: 'You're not that ugly.'

Actor: 'Whenever I perform my audiences are glued to their seats.'
Critic: 'That's the only way you can keep them in the theatre.'

'Wally Wellington is so thick he sits at the back of the bus to get a longer ride.'

Girl: 'What are you going to give me for Christmas?'
Smart Alec: 'Close your eyes and tell me what you see.'
Girl: 'Nothing.'
Smart Alec: 'That's what I'm getting you for Christmas.'

Mary: 'I spend hours looking in the mirror and admiring my good looks. Do you think that's vanity?'
Smart Alec: 'No, imagination.'

'A boy went into a cafe and ordered a can of lemonade. He took a can opener from his pocket, opened the can and drank the lemonade. He then bought another can of lemonade, used the can opener to open it and drank the lemonade. The girl behind the counter asked why he didn't use the ring pull to open the can and he replied, 'Oh, I thought that was only for people who didn't have a can opener with them.'

Diner: 'Has the chef got pigs' feet?'
Waiter: 'I can't tell, sir. He's got his shoes on.'

Woman: 'If you were my husband I'd poison your coffee.'
Man: 'And if you were my wife I'd drink it.'

Boy: 'You've got a sweet face.'
Girl: 'Do you really think so?'
Boy: 'Yes, it looks like a humbug.'

Waiter: 'Looks like rain today.'
Diner: 'Yes, but it still smells like coffee.'

'My girlfriend puts on her make up so thick that two minutes after she's stopped laughing her face is still smiling.'

* REMINDER TO GENERAL PUBLIC - ALL EXTRA JOKES (THE BEST) - ARE SUPPLIED BY STARVING ARTIST!

Ageny: 'Good news! I've booked your performing pigeons for an eight week tour.'
Performer: 'You're too late. I've eaten the act.'

Alan: 'I want to buy my girlfriend a present. What do you think she'll like?'
Smart Alec: 'Does she like you?'
Alan: 'Oh, yes. I'm positive she likes me.'
Smart Alec: 'Well, if she likes you she'll like anything.'

'It's not fair, all the kids at school call me "big head".'
'Don't worry, there's nothing in it.'

He's such a bore that even his shadow stays as far away from him as it can.

Customer: 'I'd like some poison for rats.'
Chemist: 'Have you tried Boots.'
Customer: 'I want to poison them, not kick them to death.'

'Knock! Knock!'
'Who's there?'
'Scott.'
'Scott who?'
'Scott nothing to do with you.'

As he was walking along the street the vicar saw a little girl trying to reach a high door knocker. Anxious to help, the vicar went over to her. 'Let me do it, dear,' he said, rapping the knocker vigorously.

'Great!' said the girl, 'Now run like hell!'

Sister: 'How did Mum know you didn't have a bath?'
Smart Alec: 'I forgot to wet the soap.'

'The local band ought to be.
'Ought to be what?'
'Banned.'

'It looks as if a storm is brewing, you'd better stay for dinner.'

'Oh, I don't think it will be that bad.'

Teacher: 'Our school cook has been cooking for twenty years.'
Smart Alec: 'She should be done by now.'

He's such a liar that even if he told you he was lying you wouldn't believe him.

FIRST PRIZE TO
A MOLYNEW OF CAMBRIDGE!

OXFORD - YOU CHUMP!

OKAY - OXFORD YOU CHUMP!

OK SOCK - WHAT DID HE GIVE YOU TO WIN ?

'Did you hear about the stupid shoplifter?'
'He stole a free sample.'

'Are you positive?'
'Only fools are positive.'
'Are you sure?'
'I'm positive.'

'My brother is so dim he can't count up to twenty without taking his shoes off.'

Teacher: 'As you know, the law of gravitation explains how we manage to stay on the ground.'
Pupil: 'Yes, but how did people stay on the ground before the law was passed?'

Mother: 'Alec, I wish you'd be a good boy.'
Smart Alec: 'I'll be good for 75p.'
Mother: 'Why can't you be like your father? Good for nothing.'

Mother: 'Did you thank Mrs Smith for her lovely party?'
Smart Alec: 'No, another boy did and she said, "Don't mention it" — so I didn't.'

'Did you hear about the idiot who bought a zebra and called it Spot?'

'Knock! Knock!'
'Who's there?'
'Lionel.'
'Lionel who?'
'Lionel get you nowhere.'

The school play had a happy ending — everybody was happy when it ended.

'Why did the idiot put his bed in the fireplace?'
'He wanted to sleep like a log.'

Are you a man or a mouse? Come on, squeak up.

Smart Alec: 'Waiter, do you have fried liver, boiled brains and stewed kidneys?'
Waiter: 'Yes, sir.'
Smart Alec: 'Well, you'd better go and see your doctor.'

'The nearest you'll ever get to a brainstorm is a light drizzle.'

Actor: 'I gave a brilliant performance last night. Everyone was moved . . . '
Critic: 'Yes, to the nearest exit.'

Smart Alec: 'What's a donkey's favourite food?'
Bert: 'Hay.'
Smart Alec: 'Well, you ought to know.'

'The longest I've known anything to stay in your head is an hour — and that was a cold.'

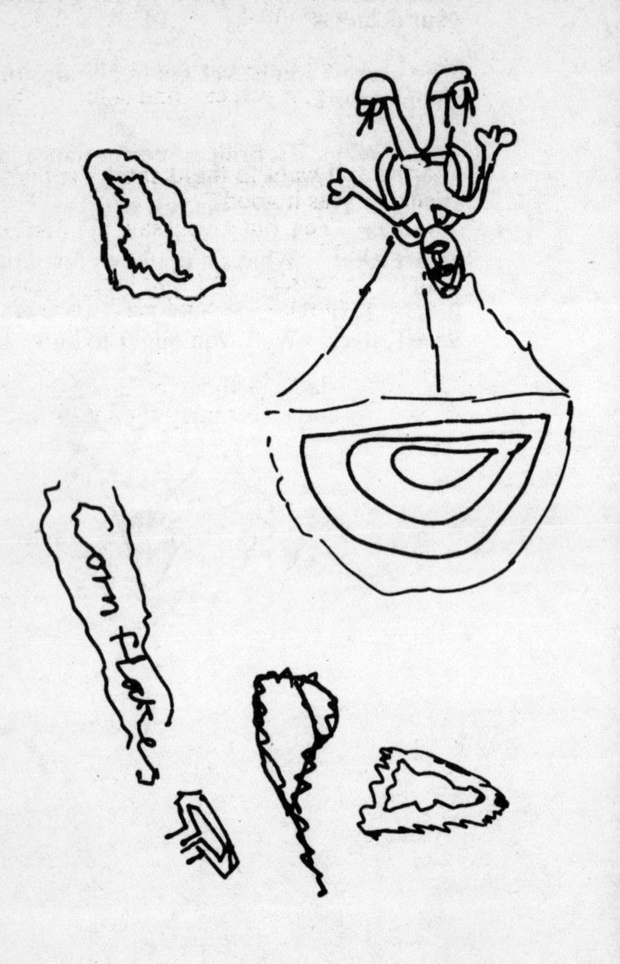

'I've got an idea.'
'Look after it. It's a long way from home.'

In this modern world you have to be crazy or else you'd go nuts!

Boy: 'Can I have this dance?'
Girl: 'Sure, if you can find someone to dance with.'

Bertha: 'I went to the theatre last night.'
Bella: 'Was it good?'
Bertha: 'Yes, but I only saw the first act, not the second.'
Bella: 'I couldn't wait that long. It said on the programme — second act, two years later.'

'When it's dad's birthday he takes the day off. When it's mum's birthday she takes several years off.'

BOO

'My sister is so dumb she thinks blood vessels are some kind of ships.'

'You'll drive me to my grave.'
'Well, you didn't expect to walk, did you?'

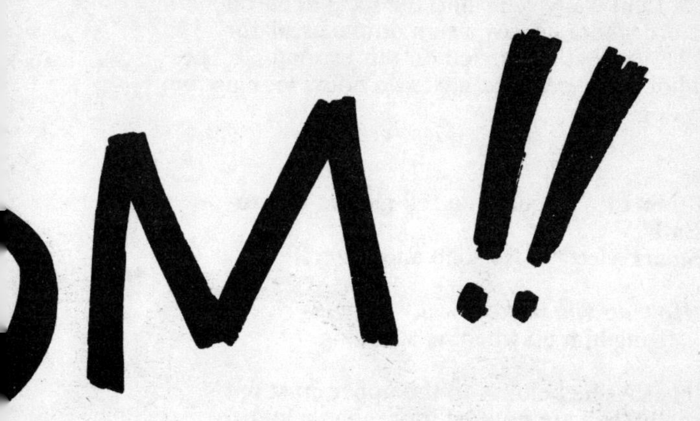

Auntie: 'You're very quiet today, Alec.'
Smart Alec: 'That's because Dad has given me 50p not to say anything about your ugly face.'

'A right wally went into the local department store where he saw a sign on the escalator "Dogs must be carried on this escalator". The idiot then spent the next two hours looking for a dog.'

Motorist: 'Could you tell me the way to Bath?'
Smart Alec: 'Usc soap and water.'

'How do you make a wally burn his ear?'
'Ring him up when he's ironing.'

'He says he belongs to the upper crust but really they are nothing more than a lot of crumbs stuck together with dough.'

Trader: 'Care to buy a nice letter opener, sir?'
Man: 'I don't need one, I'm married.'

Smart Alec: 'Do you know anything about apes?'
Bert: 'My dad raised a monkey once.'
Smart Alec: 'You're telling me!'

Boy: 'You look like my favourite film star?'
Girl: 'Really? Who's that?'
Boy: 'King Kong.'

Sports Master: 'You'd be a good footballer if it wasn't for two things.'
Smart Alec: 'What are they?'
Sports Master: 'Your feet!'

'Cynthia's teacher calls Cynthia a miracle worker — it's a miracle if she works.'

'Did you hear about the wally who went bankrupt selling lucky charms?'

Smart Alec: 'What are you going to do when you leave school?'
Wally: 'I'm going to live on my wits.'
Smart Alec: 'Well, half a living is better than none.'

'My sister is so dumb she thinks a buttress is a female goat.'

Smart Alec: 'Do you have holes in your underpants?'
Teacher: 'No, of course not!'
Smart Alec: 'Well, how do you get your feet through?'

'How does an idiot call for his dog?'
'He puts two fingers in his mouth and then shouts "Rover".'

Girl: 'Why do you call me "Angel"?'
Boy: 'Because you're always harping on about something.'

'It's obvious that animals are smarter than humans. Put eight horses in a race and twenty thousand people will go along to see it. But put eight people in a race and not one horse will bother to go along and watch.'

Mother: 'I'm a woman of few words. If I beckon with my finger it means "come here".'
Smart Alec: 'Suits me, mum. I'm a man of few words, myself. If I shake my head from side to side it means I'm not coming.'

Smart Alec: 'Your face ought to be on a magazine cover.'
Girl: 'Which one do you think? *Modern Beauty? Glamour Monthly? Good Looks Gazette?*'
Smart Alec: 'No, *Plumbers' Weekly.*'

'How do you keep flies out of the kitchen?'
'Put a bucket of manure in the lounge.'

'Did you hear about the idiot who won the Tour de France?'
'He did a lap of honour.'

'What British city has the most ignorant people?'
'London, because that is where the population is most dense.'

'Knock! Knock!'

'Who's there?'

'Ivor.'

'Ivor who?'

'Ivor a good mind not to tell you.'

Diner: 'Waiter, this soup is cold. Bring me some that's hot.'

Waiter: 'Do you want me to burn my thumb?'

'I could be a successful author if I had the mind to try it.'

'Yes, the only thing missing is the mind.'

'How does your head feel today?'

As good as new.'

'It should feel as good as new — it's never been used.'

'My sister is so stupid she thinks that aroma is someone who travels a lot.'

Smart Alec: 'I'd like to buy a dog. How much do they cost?'
Petshop Owner: 'Ten pounds a piece.'
Smart Alec: 'How much for a whole one?'

'How did the baker get an electric shock?'
'He stood on a bun and a currant ran up his leg.'

Customer: 'This restaurant must have a very clean kitchen.'
Waiter: 'Yes, sir it has. But how did you know?'
Customer: 'All the food tastes of soap.'

'Did you hear about the idiotic goalkeeper who saved a penalty but let it in on the action replay?'.

'I think my teacher must be pretty old. He told us today that he used to teach Shakespeare.'

Boy: 'Darling, how could I ever leave you?'
Girl: 'By bus, train, aeroplane, hovercraft, bicycle, rickshaw . . . '

'What's the difference between a kangaroo, a lumberjack and a bag of peanuts?'

'A kangaroo hops and chews and a lumberjack chops and hews.'

'Yes, but what's the bag of peanuts for?'

'For monkeys like you.'

Father: 'This suit fits me like a glove.'
Smart Alec: 'Yes, a boxing glove.'

Mother: 'Alec, are you teaching the parrot to swear?'
Smart Alec: 'No, mum. I'm just telling him what not to say.'

Bert was dangling a fishing rod down a manhole. The vicar gave him 50p and asked with a smile 'How many have you caught today?'

'You're the sixth,' said Bert.

'Is it true that married men live longer than single men?'

'No, it just seems longer.'

'Here I am bright and early.'

'Well, you're early.'

'My friend is so stupid he thinks that an autograph is a chart showing sales figures for cars.'

'How would a cannibal describe a man in a hammock?'

'Breakfast in bed.'

'I can't stop telling lies.'

'I don't believe you.'

Smart Alec: 'Can I have a return ticket, please.'
Railway Clerk: 'Where to?'
Smart Alec: 'Why, back here, of course.'

'A tourist stood at the top of London's Post Office Tower looking down at the ground below. "Do people fall from here often?" he asked the guide.

"Only once." replied the guide.'

'Did you hear about the idiot who made his chickens drink boiling water? He thought they'd lay hard-boiled eggs.'

'When were you born?'

'The day after they took my mother into the maternity hospital.'

'Intelligence reigns supreme in my family.'

'You must have been born during a dry spell.'

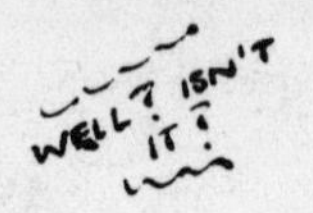

'Our librarian is so stupid she thinks that an autobiography is a book about the life story of a car.'

Eddy's father called up to him: 'Eddy, if you don't stop playing that trumpet I think I'll go crazy.'
'I think you are already,' replied Eddy 'I stopped playing half an hour ago.'

'Did you hear about the wally who hijacked a submarine?'
'He demanded a million pounds and a parachute.'

Waiter: 'And how did you find your meat, sir?'
Customer: 'Oh, I just lifted a chip and there it was.'

'What is written at the top of an idiot's ladder?'
'Stop.'

Teacher: 'Alec, stop showing off. Do you think you're the teacher of this class?'
Smart Alec: 'No, sir.'
Teacher: 'Well stop behaving like a fool.'

'Did you hear about the wally who poured whisky on his lawn?'
'He thought it would come up half cut.'

'I was born in London.'

'Funny things happen in Birmingham as well.'

'Why is it that when I stand on my head the blood rushes to my head but when I stand on my feet the blood doesn't rush to my feet?'

'Your feet aren't empty.'

Smart Alec: 'Tell me, Grandad, can you make a noise like a frog?'
Grandad: 'Why?'
Smart Alec: 'Because Dad says when you croak we'll inherit all your money.'

'Why did the burglar cut the legs off his bed?'
'Because he was advised to lie low for a while.'

A woman telephoned her local newspaper to let them know that she had just given birth to eighteen children. The reporter didn't quite hear the message and said, 'Would you repeat that?'
'Not if I can help it,' replied the woman.

'How do you keep an idiot happy for hours?'
'Give him a piece of paper with PTO written on both sides.'

'Why is a red-headed idiot like a biscuit?'
'Because he's a ginger nut.'

Smart Alec: 'If frozen water is iced water what is frozen ink?'
Bill: 'Iced ink.'
Smart Alec: 'You certainly do!'

Smart Alec: 'When were you born?'
Wally: 'April 2nd.'
Smart Alec: 'A day too late.'

I'm nobody's fool.
Perhaps you could get someone to adopt you.

'My Dad thinks that blackmail is post that's been delivered down a chimney.'

Never buy a cheap violin. It might be a fiddle.

Smart Alec: 'Haven't I seen you somewhere before?'
Film Star: 'You may have seen me at the pictures.'
Smart Alec: 'That's possible. Where do you usually sit?'

'*Did you hear about the wally who bought a paper shop?*'
'It blew away.'

'Why did the idiot give up his attempt to cross the Channel on a plank?'

'He couldn't find a plank that was long enough.'

Beautician: 'Did that mud pack I gave you for your wife improve her appearance?'
Man: 'It did for a while — then it fell off.'

Teacher: 'How old do you think I am?'
Smart Alec: 'Forty-six.'
Teacher: 'What makes you think that?'
Smart Alec: ''Cos my brother is twenty-three and he's only half nuts.'

'I'm not myself today.'
'Yes, I noticed the improvement.'

'My brother thinks that a blazer is a jacket that's on fire.'

'I do wish you wouldn't go around telling everyone I'm a bore.'
'Sorry, I didn't know it was a secret.'

Did you hear about the idiotic Sea Scout?
His tent sank.

Smart Alec (to greengrocer): 'One pound of mixed nuts please — and not too many coconuts.'

First Idiot: 'Have you seen today's newspaper?'
Second Idiot: 'No. Why, what was in it?'
First Idiot: 'My lunch.'

'What is black, gushes out ot the ground and shouts "Excuse me"?'
'Refined oil.'

'My dad is so short-sighted he can't get to sleep unless he counts elephants.'

Smart Alec: 'I think you're a nice bird.'
Girlfriend: 'I must be a bird for you're certainly a worm.'

My girlfriend thinks I'm a great wit.
Well, she's half right.

'My sister thinks that a bulldozer is a sleeping bull.'

Father: 'When I was your age I thought nothing of walking to school.'
Smart Alec: 'I don't think much of it, either.'

'One day Alec answered his front door to find a dirty old tramp standing there. "You look a kindly lad." said the tramp. "I haven't had a bite all week."

So Alec bit him.'

Piano Tuner: 'I've come to tune your piano.'
Man: 'But I didn't send for you.'
Piano Tuner: 'No, your neighbours did.'

Footballer: 'Why do you call me "Cinderella"?'
Trainer: 'Because you're always missing the ball.'

'Statistics say that one in four people is mentally ill. So check your friends — if three of them seem okay, you're the one.'

Smart Alec: 'Why didn't you answer?'
Wally: 'I did — I shook my head.'
Smart Alec: 'I didn't hear it rattle.'

'My mother is a bit daft. She thinks that a catastrophy is a cup awarded at a cat show.'

Auntie: 'I have the face of a sixteen-year-old girl.
Smart Alec: 'Well, you'd better give it back. You're getting it all wrinkled.'

Did you hear about the idiot who had a new bath put in? The plumber said, 'Would you like a plug for it?'
The idiot replied, 'Oh, I didn't know it was electric.'

'Did you hear about the vicar who turned up at the wrong funeral?'
'He made a grave mistake.'

'Doctor, doctor I keep talking to myself.'
'I wondered why you were looking so bored.'

'Are you or your sister the oldest in the family?'

'Neither, Mum and Dad are older than both of us.'

'I've got a good idea.'

'Must be beginner's luck.'

'I was doing my homework yesterday and I asked my dad what a circle is. He said it's a round straight line with a hole in the middle.'

HOI! - LEAVE
US LINES OUT
OF THIS

'How do you make an idiot laugh on Saturday?'

'Tell him a joke on Friday.'

First Wally: 'My family think I'm crazy because I like sausages.'
Second Wally: 'There's nothing crazy about that. I like sausages, too.'
First Wally: 'You do? Then you must come round to see my collection, I've got hundreds.'

'Did you hear about the idiot who decided to listen to the match? He burned his ear.'

Father: 'I wonder how long a man can live without a brain.'
Smart Alec: 'How old are you?'

First Idiot: 'This match won't light.'
Second Idiot: 'What's wrong with it?'
First Idiot: 'I don't know. It worked a moment ago.'

'Wally Nutcase was asked to describe the Cheddar Gorge. He said it was a giant cheese sandwich.'

Dentist: 'What sort of filling would you like to have in your tooth?'
Smart Alec: 'Chocolate.'

How would you make a cannonball?
  Step on his foot outside the church.

Diner: 'Waiter, what on earth is this?'
Waiter: 'It's bean soup, sir.'
Diner: 'I don't care what it's been, I want to know what it is now.'

'What do you get when you cross an idiot with a watch?'
  'A cuckoo clock.'

'Waiter, do you serve crabs?'
'Sit down, sir. We serve anybody.'

'If your nose runs and your feet smell, what is wrong with you?'
'You were built upside-down.'

'My dad has such a long face the barber charges him twice for shaving it.'

Smart Alec: 'I think we are intellectual opposites.'
Ben: 'What do you mean?'
Smart Alec: 'I'm intellectual and you're the opposite.'

'My dad is stupid. He thinks a fjord is a Norwegian motor car.'

When can you tell that someone has a glass eye?
When it comes out in conversation.

Wally Woollynut was given the job of painting a flagpole but he didn't know how much paint he would need. 'Lay it down and measure it,' suggested a mate.
'That's no good,' said Wally, 'I need to know the height, not the length.'

Diner: 'Waiter, there's only one piece of meat on my plate.'
Waiter: 'Just a moment, sir and I'll cut it in two.

Bill: 'What makes you think your Mum wants you to leave home?'
Smart Alec: 'Every day she wraps my lunch in a road map.'

'You are so ugly your face would stop a clock.'
'And yours would make one run.'

'You must think I'm a perfect idiot.'
'No, you're not perfect.'

'My sister thinks that a juggernaut is an empty beer mug.'

Mary: 'Last night I dreamed I was with the world's most handsome man.'
Smart Alec: 'What was I wearing?'

An idiot telephoned London Airport. 'How long does it take to get to New York?'

'Just a minute.'

'Thanks very much.'

Farmer: 'Baa, baa, black sheep, have you any wool?'
Sheep: 'What do you think this is you stupid idiot, nylon?'

Father: 'Don't you know it's rude to reach across the table for the cakes? Haven't you got a tongue?'
Smart Alec: 'Yes, but my arm's longer!'

Wife: 'Did you know that most accidents happen in the kitchen?'
Husband: 'I know — I have to eat them.'

'There's a man outside with a funny face.'
'Tell him I've already got one.'

First Man: 'I'm going to shoot you because I vowed that if ever I saw someone who looks like me I'd shoot them.'
Second Man: 'Do I look like you?'
First Man: 'Yes.'
Second Man: 'Then shoot.'

'Did you hear about the scientist who was so absent-minded that when he went to work he slammed his wife and kissed the door?'

Girl: 'Why do you call me your melancholy baby?'
Boy: 'Because you've got a head like a melon and a face like a collie.'

'Knock! Knock!'
'Who's there?'
'Lemmy.'
'Lemmy who?'
'Lemmy in, it's freezing out here.'

'What is yellow and stupid?'
'Thick custard.'

'Knock! Knock!'
'Who's there?'
'Olive.'
'Olive who?'
'Olive here, so let me in.'

'Did you hear about the stupid jellyfish? — It set.'

First Idiot: 'Time hangs heavily on my hands these days.'
Second Idiot: 'Then why don't you get a wristwatch instead of that grandfather clock you're wearing?'

Smart Alec: 'I'm homesick.'
Dan: 'But this is your home.'
Smart Alec: 'I know, and I'm sick of it.'

Drowning Man: 'Help! Help! I can't swim.'
Smart Alec: 'So what? I can't play the piano.'

Dopey: 'I'm writing a letter to my girlfriend.'
Drippy: 'Don't be stupid. You can't write.'
Dopey: 'That's all right. My girlfriend can't read.'

Smart Alec: 'If you give me one of your sweets I'll tell you how to make them last longer.'
Gail: 'Here you are, then . . . now tell me.'
Smart Alec: 'Suck them with the wrappers on.'

'Why did the idiot wear two suits to the fancy dress party? He went as twins.'

My sister is so bowlegged dad hangs her on the back door for luck.

Fred: 'What does your Dad do for a living?'
Smart Alec: 'He collects fleas.'
Fred: 'What does your Mum do?'
Smart Alec: 'She scratches.'

'What happened to the butcher who backed into a meat slicer? He got behind with his work.'

First Woman: 'Whenever I'm down in the dumps I buy myself a new hat.'
Second Woman: 'Oh, so that's where you get them!'

Smart Alec: 'You have two beautiful eyes.'
Girlfriend: 'Thank you very much.'
Smart Alec: 'It's a pity they don't match.'

'This morning I felt that today was going to be my lucky day. I got up at seven, had seven pounds in my pocket, there were seven of us at lunch and there were seven horses in the seven o'clock race — so I backed the seventh.'

Did it win?'

'No, it came in seventh.'

Smart Alec: 'What did my brain X-ray show?'
Doctor: 'Nothing.'

Charlie: 'I throw myself into everything I undertake.'
Smart Alec: 'Why don't you go and dig a deep well?'

'I'm speechless.'
'Good, just stay that way.'

'Where do fleas go in the winter?'
'Search me!'
'No thanks.'

* ANOTHER BRILLIANT OFF THE CUFF JOKE BY STARVING ARTIST!

Fred: 'Our dog is just like one of the family.'
Smart Alec: 'Which one?'

'Did you hear about the florist who had two children? One's a budding genius and the other's a blooming idiot.'

Neil: 'I've changed my mind.'
Smart Alec: 'About time, too. Does the new one work any better?'

Girl: 'Did you like that cake Mrs Jones?'
Visitor: 'Yes, very much.'
Girl: 'That's funny. My mum said you didn't have any taste.'

Two shark fishermen were sitting on the side of their boat just off the coast of Florida, cooling their feet in the sea. Suddenly an enormous shark swam up and bit off one fisherman's leg. 'A shark's bitten off my leg,' yelled the fisherman.

'Which one?' asked his friend.

'I don't know,' replied the first, 'When you've seen one shark you've seen 'em all.'

Teacher: 'Alec, I'm talking to you. Didn't you hear me?'
Smart Alec: 'Yes, sir. But yesterday you told me not to answer back.'

At the inquest into her husband's death by food poisoning Mrs Wally was asked by the coroner if she could remember her husband's last words. 'Yes,' she replied. 'He said "I don't know how that shop can make a profit from selling this salmon at only twenty pence a tin . . . "'

Psychiatrist: 'Well, what's your problem?'
Patient: 'I prefer brown shoes to black shoes.'
Psychiatrist: 'There's nothing wrong with that. Lots of people prefer brown shoes to black shoes. I do myself.'
Patient: 'Really? How do you like yours, fried or boiled?'

'Why did the stupid pilot land his plane on a house? Because the landing lights were on.'

Smart Alec: 'Do you feel like a cup of tea?'
Father: 'Yes, I do.'
Smart Alec: 'I thought so, You look wet and sloppy!'

Teacher: 'Why weren't you at school yesterday?'
Smart Alec: 'I was sick, sir.'
Teacher: 'How come you are always off sick when Rovers play?'
Smart Alec: 'Because the way Rovers play is enough to make anyone sick.'

'Did you hear about the idiot who found some milk bottles in a field? He thought he'd found a cow's nest.'

Smart Alec: 'You remind me of the deep blue sea.'
Girlfriend: 'Do you mean because I'm so restless and romantic?'
Smart Alec: 'No, you just make me feel sick.'

Headmaster: 'This is the third time I've had to cane you this week. What have you got to say to that?'
Smart Alec: 'Thank goodness it's Friday.'

You are such a bore. You are always talking when I want you to listen.

Imagine that poor little brain all alone in that great big head.

Mother: 'Keep that dog out of the house. It's full of fleas.'
Smart Alec: 'Keep out of the house, Rover. It's full of fleas.'

'Why did the stupid sailor grab a bar of soap when his ship sank? He thought he could wash himself ashore.'

'Don't worry if your job is small,
And your rewards are few.
Remember that the mighty oak
Was once a nut like you.'

Teacher: 'Alec, you're late again. Don't you know what time we start school?'
Smart Alec: 'No, you've always started before I arrive.'

'Some people say the school cook's cooking is out of this world. Most pupils wish it was out of their stomachs.'

‘My auntie Mabel has got so many double chins it looks like she is peering over a pile of crumpets.’

‘I used to be a seven stone weakling,’ said Marty Musclebound to a friend, ‘And when I went on the beach with my girlfriend a twelve-stone bully kicked sand in my face. I decided to take a body building course and after a lot of work I eventually got my weight up to twelve stone and I was full of muscle power.’

‘That’s great!’ exclaimed his friend.

‘No it wasn’t,’ moaned Marty, ‘Next time I went on the beach a fifteen-stone bully kicked sand in my face!’

‘Knock! Knock!’

‘Who’s there?’

‘Bella.’

‘Bella who?’

‘Bella not working, that’s why I knocka.’

'The school cook's cooking is so bad the school dustbins have ulcers.'

'If you watch the way that many motorists drive you will soon reach the conclusion that the most dangerous part of a car is the nut behind the wheel.'

Barber: 'Was your tie red when you came in here?'
Customer: 'No.'
Barber: 'Oh, crikey!'

Man: 'I think I've seen your face somewhere else.'
Smart Alec: 'I don't think so. It's always been here on me.'

'Knock! Knock!'
'Who's there?'
'A Malayan.'
'A Malayan who?'
'A Malayan down on the door step.'

Man: 'I used to be in the circus.'
Smart Alec: 'Really? Which cage?'

At three o'clock one morning a veterinary surgeon was woken from a deep sleep by the ringing of his telephone. He staggered downstairs and answered the 'phone. 'I'm sorry if I woke you,' said a voice at the other end of the line.

'That's all right,' said the vet, 'I had to get up to answer the 'phone, anyway.'

There's a large crack in the sitting room of Jimmy's house so he goes around telling everyone that he's from a broken home.

'What happened to the man who couldn't tell the difference between porridge and putty? All his windows fell out.'

'*Knock! Knock!*'
'Who's there?'
'*Percy.*'
'Percy who?'
'*Percy-vere and you may find out.*'

SMATTERSTHWAIT?
NO!
CRUMBLES?
NO!
JIMPSON?
NOPE!
SMITH?
NO!
PINGLES?
NO!
DAWLISH-PUNGLETHORPE-SWAINSON?
YES!!!

'Why is your mum covered with bandages?'
'She had a terrible accident. She was having her face lifted and the crane broke.'

'My auntie Edna is so fat uncle Tom has to stand up in bed each morning to see if it's daylight.'

Tommy: 'What makes you think I'm stupid?'
Smart Alec: 'Because when you went in to see that mind reader just now he only charged you half price.'

Smart Alec likes going to the cinema but he believes that the trouble with most films is that they shoot too much film and not enough actors.

'What happened to the optician who fell into the lens grinding machine?'

'He made a spectacle of himself.'

'Knock! Knock!'

'Who's there?'

'Chester.'

'Chester who?'

'Chester minute and I'll take a look.'

'You think you are clever but really you're just a wally. You are like a piece of blotting paper. You soak everything in — but you get it all backwards.'

Alec's latest girlfriend reminds him of the Venus de Milo — beautiful, but not all there.

Dan: 'Did you say your grandmother spreads happiness wherever she goes?'
Smart Alec: 'No, I said whenever she goes.'

'Three men go into a car wash. Which one is the idiot?'
'The one on the motorbike.'

'Knock! Knock!'
'Who's there?'
'Archibald.'
'Archibald who?'
'Archibald for your age?'

My mother talks so much that when she goes on holiday she spreads sunburn lotion on her tongue.

Today she is so tired she can hardly keep her mouth open.

First Cowboy: 'Why did that Indian call me paleface?'
Second Cowboy: 'Because you've got a face like a bucket.'

'Why did the man put his wife under the bed?'

'Because he thought she was a little potty.'

'Knock! Knock!'
'Who's there?'
'Jeff.'
'Jeff who?'
'Jeff fancy opening the door?'

'Don't scratch your head, you might get a splinter in your finger.'

The ceilings of our holiday hotel were so thin you could get sunburnt without leaving the room.

And the rooms were so small the mice had round shoulders.

'Say, you've got something there — let's hope it isn't catching.'

'Did you hear about the wally who wanted to water ski? Eventually he gave up the idea because he couldn't find a sloping lake.'

'How can you join the police?'
'Handcuff them together.'

Teacher: 'How many feet are there in a yard?'
Smart Alec: 'Depends how many people are in the yard.'

'My little brother is so inquisitive he once took his nose apart to see what makes it run.'

'My dad lost his last job through illness — the boss got sick of him.'

Uncle Scrooge is so mean that if he was a ghost he wouldn't give you a fright.

Psychiatrist: 'I am pleased to say, Mr Twit that after your five weeks treatment you do not have an inferiority complex.'
Mr Twit: 'Really?'
Psychiatrist: 'No, you really are inferior.'

'What happened to the stupid bookworm?'
'It died in a brick.'

'How do you keep an idiot in suspense?'
'I'll tell you next week.'

Smart Alec: 'I think you are stupid. Do you know why?'
Tommy: 'I can't think.'
Smart Alec: 'That's right!'

'My sister's nose is so turned up everytime she sneezes she blows her hat off.'

'What is small, pink, wrinkly, and belongs to Grandpa?'
'Grandma.'

'My mother uses lemon juice for her complexion. Maybe that is why she always looks so sour.'

'Where is the dead centre of Birmingham?'
'The cemetery.'

Jane's father decided to take all the family out to a restaurant for a meal. As he'd spent quite a lot of money for the meal he said to the waiter 'Could I have a bag to take the leftovers home for the dog?'

'Gosh!' exclaimed Jane, 'Are we getting a dog?'

'How do you confuse an idiot?'

'Give him two spades and ask him to take his pick.'

'At our local restaurant you can eat dirt cheap — but who wants to eat dirt?'

Smart Alec: 'When my dad was in China he saw a woman hanging from a tree.'
Teacher: 'Shanghai?'
Smart Alec: 'No, only a few feet off the ground.'

'Our headmaster is going out of his mind — and his mind is glad he's leaving.'

Smart Alec: 'How much are those apples?'
Greengrocer: 'Fifty pence a pound.'
Smart Alec: 'That's too much for me.'
Greengrocer: 'Well, you could have half a pound for thirty pence.'
Smart Alec: 'In that case I'll take the other half for twenty pence.'

'That man's moustache and my dog go to the same vet.'

Smart Alec was walking along the road when he saw a man trip over a paving stone. 'Stupid, git,' said Alec.

'Come here,' said the man, 'I'll teach you to use language like that.'

'Too late,' said Alec 'My dad's taught me already.'

'My brother thinks he is a chicken.'

'Why don't you take him to the doctor and have him cured?'

'We need the eggs.'

'Did you hear about the man who slept with his head under the pillow? When he awoke in the morning the fairies had taken all his teeth.'

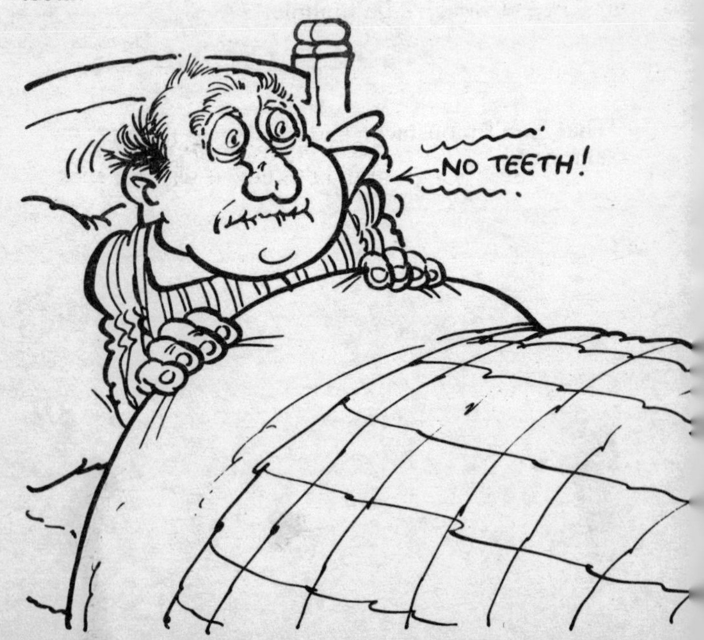

Girl: 'I want to get a dress to match my eyes.'
Smart Alec: 'There aren't many shops that sell bloodshot dresses.'

When Ben hit his thumb with a hammer he let out a few choice words. Shocked by her son's outburst, his mother said, 'Don't you dare use that kind of language in here.'

'William Shakespeare did,' replied Ben.

'Well, you'd better stop going around with him,' said mum.

Father: 'This shirt must have shrunk in the wash. The collar is so tight it's choking me.'
Mother: 'Don't be so stupid. You've got your head through a buttonhole.'

'How dare you swear in front of my wife!'

'Sorry, mate. I didn't know it was her turn.'

'The hotel we stayed in for our holiday offered bed and board but it was impossible to say which was the bed and which was the board.'

'What is a snail?'

'A slug with a crash helmet.'

'At my piano teacher's last performance the audience cheered and cheered. The piano was locked.'

‘The trouble with being punctual is that there is no-one there to appreciate it.’

Cynthia ordered a drink in a restaurant. It tasted absolutely vile so she called the waiter over and said, ‘If this is coffee please bring me some tea. But if this is tea please bring me some coffee.’

One day Bob’s mother turned to Bob’s father and said, ‘It’s such a nice day, I think I’ll take Bob to the zoo.’

‘I wouldn’t bother,’ said father, ‘If they want him let them come and get him.’

Vicar: ‘I don’t think you know anything about the Bible. Is there any passage you can quote?’
Smart Alec: ‘Yes, Judas departed and went and hanged himself.’
Vicar: ‘Very good. Do you know another?’
Smart Alec: ‘Go thou and do likewise.’

'Why is English called the Mother tongue?'
'Because Dad never gets a word in.'

Fred and his friends were making rather a lot of noise in the local cinema. Eventually a lady in front turned round to them and said, 'Do you mind? I'm trying to watch this film.'
'In that case,' said Fred, 'You're facing the wrong way.'

'What do you do if your nose goes on strike?'
'Picket.'

First Idiot: 'I've got carrots growing out of my ears.'
Second Idiot: 'Goodness! How did that happen?'
First Idiot: 'I don't know — I planted cabbages!'

'What do you get if you cross a horse with a skunk?'

'Whinny the Pooh.'

One day Tony's girlfriend wrote to him to say their friendship was off and could she have her photograph back?

Tony sent her a pile of pictures of different girls with the message, 'I can't remember what you look like. Could you please take out your photograph and return the rest?'

'Did you hear about the idiotic karate champion who joined the army? The first time he saluted he almost killed himself.'

I FORGOT MY TOWEL 'N SOAP!

'What does the Queen do when she burps?'
'She issues a royal pardon.'

Wife: 'We're having Mother for dinner, dear.'
Husband: 'I'd rather have fish and chips.'

Ben's teacher regards Ben as a wonder child. He wonders whether he'll ever learn anything.

An idiot decided to start a chicken farm so he bought a hundred chickens to start. A month later he returned to the dealer for another hundred chickens because all of the first lot had died.

A month later he was back at the dealer's for another hundred chickens for the second lot had died also. 'But I think I know where I'm going wrong,' said the idiot, 'I think I'm planting them too deep.'

Girl: 'Why do you call me "Peach"? Is it because I'm sweet and tasty?'
Smart Alec: 'No, it's because you're yellow and furry.'

Smart Alec: 'Excuse me, sir, but have you heard about the wally who is going around the school saying "No"?'
Teacher: 'No.'

TOWEL - SOAP -
SHOWER CAP - OK - WHERE'S
THAT

'When a man marries how many wives does he get? Sixteen — four richer, four poorer, four better, four worse.'

Teacher: 'If one and one makes two, and two and two make four, what do four and four make?'
Smart Alec: 'That's not fair. You do all the easy sums and give me the difficult ones.'

Lawyer (to client): 'I've managed to get you a suspended sentence . . . they're going to hang you.'

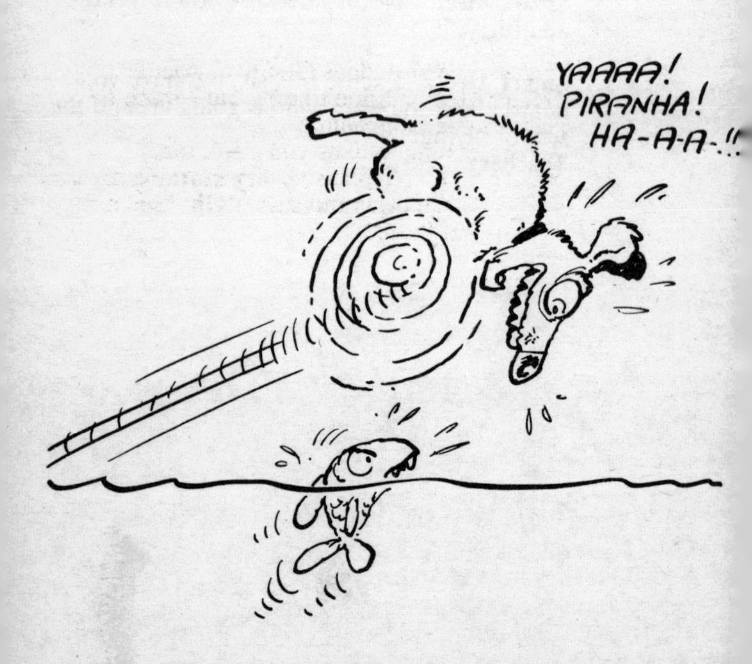

'Our kitchen is so small we can only use condensed milk.'

Vicar: 'If you found a £5 note would you keep it?'
Smart Alec: 'No, of course not.'
Vicar: 'Good boy! What would you do with it?'
Smart Alec: 'I'd spend it.'

'Stop acting like a fool.'
'Who's acting?'

Vicar: 'Where does God live, Alec?'
Smart Alec: 'I don't know but I think he lives in our bathroom.'
Vicar: 'What makes you think that?'
Smart Alec: 'Because every morning my dad bangs on the door and says, "Oh, God are you still in there?"'

'My parents were very funny about my brother's education. Only an approved school was good enough.'

Teacher: You must have a sixth sense, Alec. You certainly show no sign of the other five.

Clare's singing is improving. People are putting cotton wool in only one ear now.

'How can you cure someone of biting their nails?'

'Knock all their teeth out.'

A fat girl went into a cafe and ordered two slices of apple pie with four dollops of ice cream covered with lashings of raspberry sauce and piles of chopped nuts. 'Would you like a cherry on the top?' asked the waitress.

'No, thanks,' said the girl, 'I'm on a diet.'

Girl: 'Why do you call me "Laryngitis"?'
Smart Alec: 'Because you're a pain in the neck.'

'I don't know what it is that makes you stupid but whatever it is, it works.'

Scoutmaster: 'How can you light a fire with two sticks?'
Smart Alec: 'Make sure one of them is a match.'

'What goes through a fly's mind when it crashes into a car windscreen at 70mph?'
'Its legs.'

'My uncle is so small everytime he gets toothache he thinks he's got a corn on his foot.'

Is that a suit you are wearing or are you dancing with someone?

Roger was in a very full bus when a fat woman opposite said, 'If you were a gentleman, young man, you'd stand up and let someone else sit down.'

'And if you were a lady,' replied Roger, 'You'd stand up and let four people sit down.'

Smart Alec: 'My dog is a marvellous watch dog. If anyone comes anywhere near the house he lets us know.'
Fred: 'Why, does he growl and bark?'
Smart Alec: 'No, he crawls under my bed.'

Teacher: 'What are you going to do when you're as big as your father?'
Smart Alec: 'Go on a diet.'

Do you always talk like that or are you wearing itchy underwear?

A dustman was walking along whistling while balancing a dustbin on his head and carrying a bin on each shoulder. 'How do you manage to do that?' asked Jane.
'It's easy,' replied the dustman, 'Just put your lips together and blow.'

Mother: 'Alec, you've been fighting. You've lost your front tooth.'
Smart Alec: 'No I haven't. It's in my pocket.'

First Wally: 'What's that wooden box for?'
Second Wally: 'I'm going to use it as a pillow.'
First Wally: 'Won't it be a bit hard?'
Second Wally: 'Don't be silly! I'm going to stuff it with straw first!'

'*Doctor, doctor I keep losing my memory.*'
'When did you first notice that?'
'*When did I first notice what?*'

Tommy: 'Your sister's teeth have so many cavities in them she talks in echoes.'
Smart Alec: 'So what? Your sister's teeth stick out so much it looks like her nose is playing the piano.'

'My dad is rather tired this morning. Last night he dreamed he was working.'

THERE'S THE DOG!

'Your trousers remind me of two French towns — Toolong and Tooloose.'

Smart Alec: 'Where do you bathe?'
Dean: 'In the spring.'
Smart Alec: 'I said where, not when.'

'What's the best thing to take when you are run over?'
'The car's number.'

'Doctor, doctor I've just swallowed a fifty pence piece. What shall I do?'

'Just stay in bed until you see some change.'

Father: 'Are my indicators working?'
Smart Alec: 'Yes, no, yes, no, yes, no, yes, . . .'

Smart Alec: 'Where's your dog?'
Tommy: 'We had to have it put down?'
Smart Alec: 'Was it mad?'
Tommy: 'Well, it wasn't very pleased.'

'Doctor, doctor. This ointment makes my skin smart.'

'Rub some on your head, then.'

Auntie Maud: 'I suppose this hideous portrait is supposed to be an example of modern art?'
Smart Alec: 'It isn't a portrait. It's a mirror.'

Teacher: 'Why are you late?'
Smart Alec: 'I overslept.'
Teacher: 'My goodness — you mean you sleep at home as well?'

Teacher: 'If you add 20,567 to 23,678 and then divide by 97 what do you get?'
Smart Alec: 'The wrong answer.'